INTO THE VOID
The Coming Transhuman Transformation

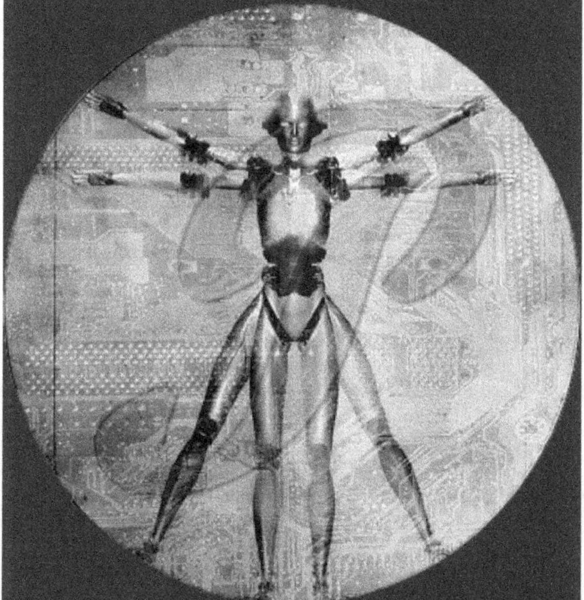

LAWRENCE J. TERLIZZESE

Christian Publishing House & Probe Ministries

INTO THE VOID

The Coming Transhuman Transformation

Lawrence J. Terlizzese

Christian Publishing House
Cambridge, Ohio

Copyright © 2016 Probe Ministries

All rights reserved. Except for brief quotations in articles, other publications, book reviews, and blogs, no part of this book may be reproduced in any manner without prior written permission from the publishers. For information, write,

support@christianpublishers.org

Unless otherwise stated, Scripture quotations are from *New American Standard Bible (NASB)* Copyright © 1960, 1962, 1963, 1968, 1971, 1972, 1973, 1975, 1977, **1995** by The Lockman Foundation

INTO THE VOID: The Coming Transhuman Transformation

ISBN-13: 978-0692744475

ISBN-10: 0692744479

Table of Contents

INTRODUCTION Into the void........................ 1

The Perfection/Failure of Technology 1

CHAPTER 1 What is Technology? 7

The Neutrality View 7

The Holistic View 8

Technology as Spirituality 10

Neutrality as Modern Myth 11

Controlling Technology 13

CHAPTER 2 Into the Void: The Coming Transhuman Transformation 15

Metaman... 17

The Singularity.. 19

Redeeming Technology 22

Technocriticism... 23

CHAPTER 3 Machinehead: From 1984 to the Brave New World Order and Beyond 26

Post-Orwellian World.. 26

The Cold War Era and *1984* 28

Brave New World Order in the 21st Century: The Imperial Machine 29

Transvaluation of Man and Machine 30

The Devil's Logic 31

CHAPTER 4 Human Enhancement and Christianity 34

Perfection and Human Enhancement................ 34

v

    Apollo as the Old Greek Ideal 35

    Eugenics and Human Enhancement................... 37

    Cyborgism 39

    Perfection in Christ 41

CHAPTER 5 Welcome to the Machine: The Transhumanist God.. 43

    Authorized Dreams Only Please!...................... 43

    You are What You Worship.............................. 44

    The Singularity Is Near 46

    The Artilect War... 47

    Ethic of Limits... 49

CHAPTER 6 The Church and the Social Media Revolution..51

    What is Social Media?....................................... 51

    The Medium Is the Message 52

    Disembodiment.. 54

    Social Media and Privacy.................................. 55

    Dialogue vs. Monologue 56

CHAPTER 7 2012: Doomsday All Over Again 58

    Progress or Regress... 58

    What the Bible Says.. 60

CHAPTER 8 "Why Does God Allow Natural Evils Such as Tsunamis, Hurricanes, and Earthquakes?" 63

Epilogue... 65

Bibliography 70

INTRODUCTION Into the void

The Perfection/Failure of Technology

Into the void, the cataclysmic crisis looming on the horizon for the 21st century concerns the exhaustion of technological innovation and the depletion of natural resources in meeting the burgeoning demands of hyper-exponential population growth – threatening to reach 9 billion souls by 2050 – the absolute limit of today's food production capacity. In the span of the next forty years population growth will demand as much food in one generation as in all human history until now.[1] Staggering!

Concomitant with population growth, the 21st century is experiencing hyper-exponential technological acceleration expected to culminate by midcentury (Circa 2045) in the so-called technological "Singularity." The twin trends of population growth and technological acceleration, the yin and the yang of modern progress controlling global history demonstrates that technological modernity has not fallen. Regressive periods in history, Philosopher Karl Jaspers, tells us was always marked by population decline and technological retardation; "At the beginning of the Dark Ages population was declining; now it has increased, and it is still increasing beyond measure. Then the menace to civilization came from without, now it comes from within. But the most conspicuous difference between our time and the third century A. D. is that then technique [technology] was stationary or retrograde, whereas now it is advancing with giant strides."[2]

---

[1] Joel K. Bourne, Jr. *The End of Plenty: The Race to feed A Crowed World* (New York: Norton, 2015), 145-162.

[2] Karl Jaspers, *Man in the Modern Age*, trans., by Eden and Cedar Paul (New York: Anchor Books, 1957), 21.

Malthusian catastrophe has been averted thus far by modern technological advances in agriculture (the Green Revolution 1970's), progress in hygiene, medicines, vaccines, etc., staying calamity by another century or less; however as the French techno-critic Jacques Ellul reminds us; "there is no such thing as overpopulation in the absolute. There is overpopulation only in relation to the possibilities of subsistence. In the long run, Malthus seems to have been right, not in an absolute sense, but in a concrete sense."[3] Demographic growth will ultimately exhaust humanity's technological ability to feed itself.

The technological Singularity will mark the completion of the Modern Project as the final limits of technological progress. Author and Inventor Ray Kurzweil stated that the nature of technological acceleration would ultimately culminate in a technological Singularity beyond which it is impossible to see; "The Singularity is technological change so rapid and so profound that it represents a rupture in the fabric of human history. Some would say that we cannot comprehend the Singularity, at least with our current level of understanding, and that it is impossible, therefore, to look past its 'event horizon' and make sense of what lies beyond." [4] Rather than raising humanity to its next evolutionary stage, and give the world *a century of progress in one hour* as promised the technological Singularity will result in the opposite, a universal regression in the human condition, and the rise of a global totalitarian dictatorship resulting in a horrendous loss of population and technological decline. Jacques Ellul mentioned this decades ago; "Technology will keep

---

[3] Jacques Ellul, *The Technological Bluff*, trans., by Geoffrey W. Bromiley (Grand Rapids: Eerdmans, 1990), 51.

[4] Ray Kurzweil, *The Law of Accelerating Returns*, 2000; http://www.kurzweilai.net/the-law-of-accelerating-returns

growing despite the noise, moral collapse, despite the costs, until the breaking limit . . . until the breakdown . . . this will not be 'zero growth' or gradual deceleration. When the accumulated effects start acting, it will be too late–i.e., it will be a catastrophe, with an enormous decline in technology and population."[5]

Just when the food crisis, resource depletion, and climate strain will be taking effect – at earth's most endangered moment technological acceleration will have reached its final limit. The point at which human survival will most need technology to relieve starvation, deprivation, end food wars between East and West, technology will fail due to the earth's exhaustion and technology's inability to advance without necessary natural resources, which has made all progress thus far possible. German Poet Friedrich Jünger noted, "As technology progresses, it devours the resources on which it depends."[6] There is a limited amount of minerals, oil, clean water, arable land, forests, etc., once these nonrenewable natural resources are spent they do not return; thus further technological progress cannot be made beyond the point of availability of natural resources necessary to fuel technological progress.

The Malthusian principle that the human population will always be greater than humanity's technological ability to sustain itself; constitutes the essence of the perfection/failure of technology; "the power of population is indefinitely greater than the power in the earth to produce subsistence for man."[7] Technology will always fail to correct the basic endemic problems of

---

[5] Jacques Ellul, *The Technological System*, trans., by Joachim Neugroschel (New York: Continuum, 1980), 288.

[6] Friedrich Georg Jünger, *The Failure of Technology* (New York: Gateway, 1949), 25.

[7] Thomas R. Malthus, *An Essay on the Principle of Population* (Amherst, New York: Prometheus Books, 1998, [1798]), 13.

mankind in a fallen spiritual condition and thus default on its promise of a "better" future; Jünger continued, "Progress in its present rapid advance creates an optical illusion, deceiving the observer into seeing things which are not there. Technology can be expected to solve all problems which can be mastered by technical means, but we must expect nothing from it which lies beyond technical possibilities."[8] The human condition remains impervious to technological progress; technology can never make better people since humanity's fundamental problem has never been a lack of technology but spiritual enlightenment; "Man does not live by bread alone, but every word that proceeds out of the mouth of God" (Matthew 4: 4).

The simple premise of this book is that despite apparent immediate gains technology makes the human plight worse through exhaustion of resources and spiritual slavery. The Singularity will mark the end of technological progress as it reaches perfection or completion without redressing the problem inherent to the human condition, hence its failure. The eminent Roman Catholic Philosopher Friedrich D. Wilhelmsen noted the juxtaposition of progress and regress; "Technology, which is an instrument for utilizing the raw material of nature, can move towards its ultimate perfection only by impoverishing nature; the less you have to work with, the more accurate and sharp must be the machinery used and the technological thinking employed. The zero of nature would be the zero of technology that had reached both its apotheosis and its death . . . the zero of human nature would be the zero of technics . . . Thus the complete perfection of technology is a contradiction. It follows, therefore, that as

---

[8] Jünger, *The Failure of Technology*, 20.

technology approaches its asymptote [singularity], it nears its own destruction."[9]

The following essays are offered as a small step away from the abyss through the rediscovery of limits in our personal and societal, technological uses and in continuity with earlier techno-critics such as Lewis Mumford, Jacques Ellul, Neil Postman, Gabriel Marcel, Martin Heidegger, Herbert Marcuse and Jean Baudrillard and C. S. Lewis; published originally as web articles and radio programs for Probe Ministries PROBE.ORG, an Evangelical apologetic ministry dedicated to addressing the pressing issues of our times with biblical answers.

(1) *What is Technology?* Attempts to define modern technology systematically and moves away from popular yet mistaken notions of technological neutrality. (2) *Into the Void* from which the book derives its title is an expose on the goals of Transhumanists who wish to push humanity into an unknown future, the Singularity or technological black hole. (3) *Machinehead* identifies the rise of the first Artilect first noted by Professor Hugo De Garis, *The Artilect War*, discussed further in chapter five. (4) *Human Enhancement and Christianity* explores the illusion of perfection driving Transhumanist aspirations. (5) *Welcome to the Machine*, identifies the technological idol and enslavement. (6) *Church and Social Media Revolution*, is a stammering attempt at the redemption of media and importance of maintaining a Christian witness in all media outlets. (7) *2012 Doomsday All Over Again* and Why *Does God Allow Natural Evil* argues that we must not get carried away with literal dates, and this includes the time of the Singularity 2045; doomsday predictions are meant to warn us and prevent doomsday not hasten it. Ultimately, humanity is responsible for the

---

[9] Friedrich D. Wilhelmsen, "Introduction" in Jünger, *The Failure of Technology*, x, xi. Ellul, The Technological Society, 85;

evil that befalls it, including our own neglect of life-sustaining technology and its composite opposite in technological burnout.

Lawrence J. Terlizzese, Ph.D.

Research Associate

Probe Ministers

CHAPTER 1 What is Technology?[10]

The Neutrality View

Most people take a favorable view towards technological progress; new cars, cell phones, and computers – what's not to like? They embrace technological innovation as a plus despite the suspicions of questionable things like cloning, genetic engineering, and nuclear weapons. But what is technology anyway? Do we really understand this all-embracing phenomenon directing human history? We often take for granted that we think we know the answer when in fact the meaning of the greatest social mover of all times remains elusive. When it comes to defining technology we are beset with the problem of defining more than just a word, but a concept and whole way of life and worldview.

The typical definition of technology these days says technology is neutral, suggesting that technology is nothing more than tools that people use as needed. Technology is a means to an end and nothing more. All objects are separate and disconnected. They are neutral and value-free, right? Tables, chairs, and light fixtures have nothing to do with each other and express no values in themselves and are completely determined by our use. They are simply objects at our disposal and present no moral problems so long as we use them for good. We can pick up a hammer and use it, then place it back in the toolbox when finished. The hammer has appropriate and inappropriate uses. Hitting nails into wood is one of the acceptable uses of a hammer; using it to play baseball is not acceptable. So long as we act as good moral agents, we use our technology rightly, or so

---

[10] July 8, 2012

https://www.probe.org/what-is-technology/

we think. This definition is so widely accepted that we have trouble ever questioning it. When faced with morally questionable uses of technology we fall back on this old cliché: "technology is neutral," and that settles all disputes. We are all familiar with this popular view and embrace it to some extent. The problem is not that the cliché is so simple or popular, but that it is so wrong. Philosophers have been telling us for decades now that the neutrality of technology definition is wrong and dangerous because it blinds us to the true nature of technology.

The Holistic View

The second view of the nature of technology, held mainly by philosophers, we call the "holistic view." This view states that the "neutral view" is false because people hold to it as a means of justifying every type of technology. The neutrality view blinds us to the true nature of technology, which is not value-free. The lack of understanding regarding the true nature of technology creates a serious problem for a society so heavily influenced by technological development. As sociologist Rudi Volti says, "This inability to understand technology and perceive its effects on our society and on ourselves is one of the greatest, if most subtle, problems of an age that has been so heavily influenced by technological change."[11] Technology is understood as a social system. We can also call it a worldview, a philosophy of life that sees all things as objects, including people. Instead of defining technology as disparate tools unconnected to each other, philosophers have suggested a more comprehensive definition that says technology does not mean neutral objects ready for use at our convenience,

---

[11] Rudi Volti, *Society and Technological Change*, 4th ed. (New York: Worth Publishers, 2001), 3.

but a way of life that informs and controls everything we do. In other words, technology is a belief system with its own worldview and agenda—more like a religion than a hammer.

This belief system is often called the *essence of technology* or *spirit of technology* and cannot be seen in technological objects because we cannot see the entire system by looking at individual parts. We must grasp the spiritual essence before we can understand its technical parts. The "neutrality view" looks only at parts rather than the whole and misses technology's true nature. This is a lot like looking at the tires of your car or its engine parts and thinking you now understand a car from seeing separate pieces of it and never seeing how the whole thing fits together.

The holistic view understands technology as a way of life and spiritual reality that shapes all our thinking. Philosopher Martin Heidegger gives the example of how the Rhine River exists not as a river, but as a source for electricity. Everything becomes stuff ready for usefulness.[12]

Technology really means an interconnected system rather than a neutral tool. The neutral definition blinds us to the true nature of technology and prevents us from mastering it. Heidegger argued that "we are delivered over to [technology] in the worst possible way when we regard it as something neutral; for this conception of it, to which today we particularity like to do homage, makes us utterly blind to the essence of technology."[13]

---

[12] Martin Heidegger, "The Question Concerning Technology" in *The Question Concerning Technology and Other Essays*, trans. by William Lovitt (New York; Harper, 1977), 16, 17.

[13] Ibid., 4.

Technology as Spirituality

The neutrality argument reassures us that we remain in control of our means rather than our means controlling us. It does not allow us to find the essence of technology in everyday technological objects such as cars, computers, or screwdrivers and baseball bats; rather, technology is a way of life and thought that creates a universal system. Technology means the grand accumulation of all the different technological parts into a global system.

Technology is a system of interlocking systems. As philosopher, Jacques Ellul said, "It is the aggregate of these means that produces technical civilization."[14] Technology is our modern frame of reference that speaks of the profoundly spiritual and not the strictly technical. If we look at individual everyday technologies, we will miss it. Instead, we must see past the common objects to the larger global system that comprises technology as a social process. In the technological system both humanity and nature have no separate standing or value outside of technical usefulness. People are simply resources to be used and discarded as needed.

This view reveals the depths to which technology shapes our thinking by informing us and conforming us into the image of the machine, which represents the greatest example of technological thinking. Everything is understood as a machine and should function as a machine including the government, the school, the church and you! Bureaucracy is a social machine.

The machine is predictable. It has no freedom. It follows mechanical steps or linear logic. Step one leads to step two, and so forth. Any deviation from its

---

[14] Jacques Ellul, *The Technological Society*, trans. by John Wilkinson (New York: Vintage, 1964), 2.

programming causes chaos and possible breakdown, which is why the machine is the worst possible analogy for human beings to follow. Yet this is the basis of the entire modern conception of life.[15] People are not machines that can be programmed; to adopt this conception reverses the role between humanity and its machines, making people conform to the image of the machine rather than vice versa. Machines are our slaves. They do what we tell them to do. They have no will, feelings or desires. Philosophers tell us that the natural relationship between people and machines is in a process of reversal so that we are becoming slaves to technology. We may control our individual use of technology, but no one as of yet controls the entire system.[16]

Neutrality as Modern Myth

Nothing can be explained by the neutrality argument, not even the meaning of "neutrality." It is simply not possible for any technology to be neutral; even the most primitive tools such as fire or stone axes take the form of their designers. Every technology bears inherent values of purpose and goals. Fire has value for a particular reason, to clear the land, cook food, keep people warm and ward off dangerous animals. By their very design, all inventions and tools reflect our values and human nature. Philosopher of Science Jacob Bronowski argued that "to quarrel with technology is to

---

[15] John Herman Randall, Jr. *The Making of the Modern Mind: A Survey of the Intellectual Background of the Present Age* (New York: Columbia University Press, 1976), 227.

[16] Lewis Mumford, *The Myth of the Machine; Technics and Human Development* (New York: Harcourt Brace Jovanovich, 1966); Idem, *The Myth of the Machine: The Pentagon of Power* (New York: Harcourt Brace Jovanovich, 1970); Neil Postman, *Technopoly: The Surrender of Culture to Technology* (New York: Knopf, 1992); Lawrence J. Terlizzese, *Hope in the Thought of Jacques Ellul* (Eugene, OR: Cascade, 2005).

quarrel with the nature of man."[17] Technology is an extension of ourselves and expresses human nature, which is never entirely good or bad, but ambivalent. Our technology reflects who we are and nothing more; it is not divine, it will not save the human race; but neither is it animal, but fully human, whose nature is always ambiguous, capable of great acts of kindness and mercy as well as cruelty and evil. People can be self-sacrificial and giving and self-destructive and greedy. There will always be good and bad effects to our inventions. They are a double-edged sword that cuts both ways, and it is our responsibility to discern between the two.

The modern bias in favor of neutrality reveals our protectionist tendencies towards all things technological. How is it that sinful people can produce morally neutral technology? We would not say that about art. "Oh! All art is morally neutral! It is all a matter of how you use it!" Yet the same creative forces go into producing technology as art. Is there anything neutral about the works of Caravaggio, Da Vinci or Picasso? Why then should there be anything neutral about Facebook or MX missiles?

This appears simple enough, but as modern people addicted to our latest toys and novelties, we have difficulty admitting we may have a problem. We don't like to think that too much Facebook might be causing young people to be further isolated from the community because they are more accustomed to relate electronically than in person, or that email actually reduces our ability to communicate because of the absence of tone of voice, body language, eye contact and personal presence. TV and film may have a surreal effect on its message, giving it a dream-like quality rather than communicating realism.

---

[17] Jacob Bronowski, "Technology and Culture in Evolution," *Philosophy of the Social Sciences* 1. 3(1971): 199.

Controlling Technology

The solution is not to abandon any of the incredible inventions of the modern age, but to recognize their limits. It is the sign of wisdom that we understand our limits and work within them. We should proceed along a two-tiered path of questioning and the application of values. Ellul said that "It is not a question of getting rid of [technology], but by an act of freedom, of transcending it."[18] The act of questioning is the first act of freedom; by becoming aware of the problem we can assert a measure of freedom and control. Through critical questioning, we recognize our limits and thus we are able to exercise a measure of control over technology.

We should develop technologies that reflect our values of freedom, equality and democracy. For example, Ellul did envision in the early 1980's the potential use of computer technology in a way that would create a decentralized source of knowledge that would maintain the values of democracy. We know this now as the internet. However, as Ellul also argued technology cannot change society for the better if we don't change ourselves. The computer can also be used to bring in stifling State control.[19] We will never have a perfect technology that has no problems, but we should be visionaries in how we think about technology and the application of our values to it.

Limits serve as a warning to us. It is obvious that society has progressed in many ways thanks to advanced technology, but society's spiritual regression shares the same condition as advancement. We have not become better people because we live in the twenty-first century

---

[18] Ellul, *The Technological Society*, xxxiii.

[19] Jacques Ellul, "New Hope for the Technological Society: An Interview with Jacques Ellul" in *Et cetera* 40.2 (1983): 192-206.

rather than the nineteenth century. Without a renewed spiritual and moral framework to direct our development and give new purpose to the system, technology may become the source of our own destruction rather than improvement. An inventory of advancement compares starkly with the litany of potential catastrophe. We have eliminated disease, but also created dangerous levels of overpopulation. We live longer and more abundant lives materially but are pushing the natural world into extinction. We are able to travel quicker and communicate instantly, contributing to world peace and understanding, but have also developed the weapons of war to unimaginable levels of devastation.

Without a moral framework to control technology and understand its ethical limits we will go down a path of losing control of technology's direction, allowing it to develop autonomously. This means it will develop in a predetermined linear direction, like a clock that will inevitably strike midnight once wound up. That direction as we have seen moves inexorably closer to the mechanization of humanity and nature. With the right value system we can begin to reassert control. The choice is yours. Where do you want to go?

CHAPTER 2 Into the Void: The Coming Transhuman Transformation[20]

In the TV show *The Six Million Dollar Man*, Lee Majors played Steven Austin, a crippled astronaut who was rehabilitated through bionic technology that gave him superhuman strength and powers. The show, like so much science fiction, presents us with the dream that technology will enhance all our facilities from sight to memory, hearing to strength, and lengthen our lifespan to boot. The bionic man represents a fictional forerunner of the transhuman transformation. The Transhumanist school believes that technology will not only enhance the human condition but eventually conquer death and grant us immortality. Human enhancement technology performs wonders in allowing the lame to walk, the blind to see, the deaf to hear and the sick to be well, but even immortality is out of the reach of technology. In striving to enhance our physical existence, we may lose our souls in the process.

In his famous book, *The Abolition of Man* published in the 1940s, C. S. Lewis wrote that modern society is one step away from "the void"[21]—"post–humanity,"[22] a state of existence from which there will be no return. Lewis argues that when we step outside of what he calls the

---

[20] December 23, 2010

https://www.probe.org/into-the-void-the-coming-transhuman-transformation/

[21] C. S. Lewis, *The Abolition of Man* (New York: Macmillan, 1947), 77.

[22] Ibid., 86.

Tao,[23] we lose all sense of value for human life that has always governed civilization. What Lewis calls the Tao, we might call Natural Law or Traditional Morality—that internal moral understanding of right and wrong which God has written on the hearts of all people (Romans 2), the *Logos* by which all things were created (John 1, see especially verse 4).[24]

In leaving traditional spiritual values behind, Lewis argues, modern technological civilization has reduced the human value to only what is natural, and we have lost our spiritual quality. Modern society has striven to conquer nature and largely succeeded, but at a great cost—with each new conquest, more losses in human dignity, more of the human spark extinguished. Lewis offers the example of eugenics from his time in the 1930's and 40's.[25] Eugenics is now a debunked science of racial manipulation and something we know was practiced with particular ferocity in Nazi Germany.[26] But the driving philosophy of manipulating nature and humanity into something new and final remains prominent. Lewis underestimated the truth of his own prophecy. He thought that maybe in 10,000 years the final leap will be taken when mankind will solidify itself into some kind of inert power structure dominated by science and technology.[27]

---

[23] Lewis, of course, did not originate this ancient Chinese concept but rather applied it to universally accessible principles.

[24] Ibid., 56.

[25] Ibid., 72

[26] See *Darwin's Racists: Yesterday, Today and Tomorrow* by Sharon Sebastian and Raymond G. Bohlin, Ph.D. Though the German Nazis acted out this hideous ideology to an extreme, eugenics was actually first promulgated in the United States, Germany and Scandinavia around the turn of the 20th Century.

[27] Lewis, *The Abolition of Man*, 71.

However, the 21st century may prove to be the era of posthumanity that Lewis foresaw in his time. The current movement of transhumanism, or human enhancement, asserts that humanity will eventually achieve a new form as a species through its adaption to modern computer technology and genetic engineering in order to reach a higher evolutionary condition. Our present state is not final. Transhumanism derives from Darwinian doctrine regarding the evolution of our species. Evolutionary forces demand that a species adapt to its environment or become extinct. On this view, many species experience a pseudo–extinction in which their adaptation gives way to another kind of species leaving its old form behind. Many evolutionists believe this happened to the dinosaurs on their way to becoming modern birds and that humanity faces the same transformation on its way up a higher evolutionary path.[28] Primates evolved into humans so humans will eventually evolve into something higher (posthuman).

Metaman

Our present condition will give way to the cyborg (which is short for cybernetic organism) as we join our bodies and minds to technological progress. Transhumanists believe that because Artificial Intelligence (computing power) advances at such a rapid pace, it will eventually exceed human intelligence and humanity will need to employ genetic engineering to modify our bodies to keep pace or become extinct. Therefore, the cyborg condition represents humanity's inevitable destiny.

The two predominant pillars in transhumanism revolve around Artificial Intelligence (AI) and genetic engineering. One represents a biological change through

---

[28] See Dr. Ray Bohlin's article PBS Evolution Series, especially the section entitled "'Great Transformations' and 'Extinction'."

manipulating genes. The other presents the merging of human intelligence with AI. The biological position (through the use of genetic engineering) claims that through the transference of genes between species, we eradicate the differences and create a global superorganism that encompasses both kinds of life—the natural and the artificial. Biophysicist Gregory Stock states that once humanity begins to tamper with its genetic code, and the codes of all other plants and animal species, that "the definition of 'human' begins to drift."[29] Through genetic engineering we will transform the human condition by merging humanity with the rest of nature, thereby creating a planetary superorganism. A superorganism operates like a beehive or an ant hill as a collection of individual organisms united as a living creature. Stock calls this Metaman, the joining of all biological creatures with machines, making one giant planetary life form. This superorganism encompasses the entire globe.

Transhumanism presupposes that no distinction exists between humanity, nature or machines. Metaman includes humanity, all it creates, and also the natural world. It acknowledges humanity's key role in the creation of farms and cities but includes all natural elements, such as forests, jungles, and weather. Metaman includes humanity and goes beyond it.[30] Stock envisions a greater role for genetic engineering in redefining biological life as different species are crossed. Humanity may now control the direction of its evolution and that of the entire planet.

---

[29] Gregory Stock, *Metaman: The Merging of Humans and Machines into a Global Superorganism* (New York: Simon and Schuster, 1993), 165.

[30] Ibid., 20.

Stock states that through "conscious design" humanity has replaced the evolutionary process.[31] This leads us to Post–Darwinism where people have supplanted the natural order with their own technological modification of humanity and the entire ecological system. "Life, having evolved a being that internalizes the process of natural selection, has finally transcended that process."[32] Humanity may now, through the agency of technological progress, seize direction of its development and guide it to wherever it wants itself to go. No other species has ever controlled its own destiny as we do.

The Singularity

A second transhumanist belief argues for the arrival of an eventual technological threshold that will be reached through the advancement of Artificial Intelligence. The argument goes like this: because AI develops at a rapid pace it will achieve equality with the human brain and eventually surpass it. Estimates as to when this will happen range from the 2020's to 2045. The evolutionary process will reach a crescendo sometime in the 21st century in an event transhumanists call "the Singularity."[33] There will be a sudden transformation of consciousness and loss of all distinction, or Singularity, between humanity and its creations, or the absence of boundaries between the natural and artificial world. Singularity watchers expect that this event will mark the ultimate merging of humans and machines. Renowned inventor and AI prophet Ray Kurzweil states, "The Singularity will allow us to transcend these

---

[31] Ibid., 228.

[32] Ibid., 231.

[33] Ray Kurzweil, *The Singularity is Near* (New York: Penguin, 2005).

limitations of our biological bodies and brains. . . . There will be no distinction, post–Singularity, between human and machine. . . ."[34] As the fictional CEO and mastermind behind a cutting edge AI company in the year, 2088 crowed, "My goal is for us to end death as we know it on earth within 50 years—for the essence of every person to live perpetually in an uploaded state. . . . The transhuman age has dawned."[35]

Both of these positions, one emanating from genetic engineering that seeks to enhance the body, the other from Artificial Intelligence that seeks to supersede and even supplant the need for bodies, argue for the eventual replacement of humanity with biological–machine hybrids. Metaman and Singularity systems are direct heirs of the modern idea of progress. They present the dawning of a technological Millennium, but they also share a long history dating back into medieval Christendom. In the early Church, technology, or the "mechanical arts," was never considered as a means to salvation or Edenic restoration. Historian David Noble argues that from Charlemagne to the early Modern period technology became associated with transcendence as the means of restoring the lost divine image or *imago dei*.[36]

Theologian Ernst Benz argues similarly that the Modern technological project was founded on a theological notion in which humanity believed itself to be the fellow worker with God in establishing His kingdom

---

[34] Ibid., 9.

[35] David Gregory, *The Last Christian*, (Colorado Springs: Waterbrook Press, 2010), 102.

[36] David F. Noble, *The Religion of Technology* (New York: Knopf, 1997), 9.

on earth through reversing the effects of the Fall.[37] We are fellow workers with God; however, this position overemphasized humanity's role in restoration to the point of becoming a works–based salvation of creation.

Despite the apparent secularity of the super science behind all the technological wonders of our time, the notions of modern progress and transhumanism remain grounded in an aberrant form of Christian theology. Noble summarizes this well when he states, "For modern technology and modern faith are neither complements nor opposites, nor do they represent succeeding stages of human development. They are merged, and always have been, the technological enterprise being, at the same time, an essentially religious endeavor."[38] The theology behind Modern technological progress remains rooted in Medieval and Early Modern notions of earthly redemption when the "useful arts,"[39] which ranged anywhere from improved agricultural methods to windmills, were invested with redemptive qualities and humanity began to assume an elevated status over nature. "In theological terms, this exalted stance vis-à-vis nature represented a forceful reassertion of an early core Christian belief in the possibility of mankind's recovery of its original God–likeness, the 'image–likeness of man to God' from Genesis (1:26), which had been impaired by sin and forfeited with the Fall."[40] Technology becomes the means of restoring the original divine image. Technological development was expected to reverse the effects of the Fall and restore original perfection. This theology also serves as the impetus behind Millennial

---

[37] Ernst Benz, *Evolution and Christian Hope: Man's Concept of the Future from Early Fathers to Teilhard de Chardin* trans., Heinz G. Frank (New York: Doubleday, 1966), 124-125.

[38] Noble, *The Religion of Technology*, 4, 5.

[39] Ibid.,14.

[40] Ibid.

thought which believes technology helps humanity recover from the Fall and leads to an earthly paradise. Transhumanism extends this Millennial belief into the twenty–first century.

Redeeming Technology

We are faced with the problem of how to redeem all the advances of technology such as human enhancement without losing ourselves in the process. Idolatry preoccupies our central concern with technology. Biblically speaking, idolatry exalts the work of humanity, including individual human beings, over God; we commit idolatry when we serve the creature rather than the Creator. "Professing to be wise, [we] became fools, and exchanged the glory of the incorruptible God for an image in the form of corruptible man and of birds and four–footed animals and crawling creatures" (Rom. 1:22-23). Theologian Paul Tillich offers a keen and insightful definition of idolatry when he states, "Idolatry is the elevation of a preliminary concern to ultimacy. Something essentially partial is boosted into universality, and something essentially finite is given infinite existence."[41] Transhumanism presents us with a spiritualization of technology believed to grant us immortality through shedding our bodies and adopting machine ones or through genetic engineering that will prolong bodily life indefinitely. Our Modern age defines technology as a source of material redemption by placing finite technical means into a divine position, thus committing idolatry.

In seeking to reconcile technology with a biblical theology, we have three possible approaches. *Technophobia* represents the first position. This view

---

[41] Paul Tillich, *Systematic Theology: Reason and Revelation Being and God*, Vol. 1 (Chicago: University of Chicago Press, 1951), 13.

contends that we should fear technological innovation and attempt to destroy it. The Unabomber Manifesto offers the most radical, pessimistic and violent expression of this position, arguing for a violent attack against the elites of technological civilization such as computer scientists in an effort to return society to primitive and natural conditions in hopes of escaping the kind of future transhumanists expect.[42] However, the entire tenor of our times moves in the opposite direction, that of *technophilism*, or the inordinate love for technology. Transhumanism optimistically believes that through technological innovation we will restore our God–like image. A third position asserts a mediating role between over–zealous optimism and radical morose pessimism.[43]

Technocriticism

Technocriticism offers the only viable theological position. By understanding technology as a modern form of idolatry, we are able to place it in a proper perspective. Technocriticism does not accept the advances of innovation and all the benefits new technology offers without critical dialogue and reflection. Technocriticism warns us that with every new invention a price must be paid. Progress is not free. With the invention of the automobile came air pollution, traffic, and accidents. Computers make data more accessible, but we also suffer from information overload and a free–flow of harmful material. Cell phones enhance communication, but also operate as an electric leash, making inaccessibility virtually impossible. Examples of the negative effects of any technology can be multiplied

---

[42] FC, *The Unabomber Manifesto: Industrial Society and Its Future* (BerkeleSee Neil Postman, *Technopoly: The Surrender of Culture to Technology* (New York: Knopf, 1992), 5.y, CA: Jolly Roger Press, 1995).

43

if we cared enough to think through all the implications of progress. Technocriticism does not allow us the luxury of remaining blissfully unaware of the possible negative consequences and limitations of new inventions. This approach is essential because it demonstrates the fallibility of all technological progress and removes its divine status.

Technocriticism humanizes technology. We assert nothing more than the idea that technology expresses human nature. Technology is us! Technology suffers the same faults and failures that plague human nature. Technology is not a means of restoring our lost divine image or reasserting our rightful place over nature. This amounts to a works–based salvation and leads to dangerous utopian and millennial delusions that amount to one group imposing its grandiose vision of the perfect society on the rest. Such ideologies include Marxism, Technological Utopianism and now Transhumanism. We are restored to the divine "image of His Son" by grace through faith alone (Rom. 8:29). Technology, serving as an extension of ourselves, means that what we create will bear our likeness, both as the image-bearers of God and in sinful human identity. It contains both positive and negative consequences that only patient wisdom can sort through.

Through criticism, we limit the hold technology has on our minds and free ourselves from its demands. We use technology but do not ascribe salvific powers of redemption to it. A critical approach becomes even more crucial the further we advance in the fields of genetic engineering and AI. We do not know where these fields will lead, and an uncritical approach that accepts them simply because it is possible to do so appears dangerous. We live under the delusion that technology frees us, but as Lewis warns, "At the moment, then, of Man's victory over Nature, we find the whole human race subjected to some individual men, and those individuals subjected to that in themselves which is purely 'natural'—to their irrational impulses."[44] The famous science-fiction writer Frank Herbert echoes Lewis's sentiments in his epic novel *Dune*: "Once men turned their thinking over to machines in the hope that this would set them free. But that only permitted other men with machines to enslave them."[45] Genetic engineering or merging humanity with AI only exchanges one condition for another. We will not reach the glorified condition transhumanists anticipate. A responsible critical approach will ask, into whose image are we transforming?

---

[44] Lewis, *The Abolition of Man*, 79, 80.

[45] Frank Herbert, *Dune* (New York: Ace, 1965), 11.

CHAPTER 3 Machinehead: From 1984 to the Brave New World Order and Beyond[46]

Wherever the survival of humanity is threatened, we find the work of Satan. In the previous century that was Fascism, then Mutually Assured Destruction during the Cold War. Today, Satan hides behind the ascendancy of the global Empire of Technology: assimilation of humanity into the machine, creating a new planetary being: the Cyborg. I believe people best understand large conglomerates when personalized, such as referring to the Federal Government as "Uncle Sam," so I have chosen to name the Brave New World Order: Machinehead!

Post-Orwellian World

Say good bye to Orwell's nightmare world of *1984!*[47] And welcome to Machinehead: the Brave New World Order and beyond!

Machinehead is what I call the technological idol or the planetary being taking shape in the convergence of human and computer intelligence, a global cyborg. "Machine" is defined as *one global system with many subsystems.*

Experts already recognize the global system as a superorganism, one life-form made of billions and billions of individual parts or cells like an anthill or beehive, with one mind and one will. Thus, the global machine consists

---

[46] September 5, 2015

https://www.probe.org/machinehead-from-1984-to-the-brave-new-world-order-and-beyond/

[47] George Orwell, *1984* {New York: HBJ, Inc., 1949}, 17)

of millions of subsystems interfacing one over-system. Mankind acts as an agent for the global machine's ascendancy, creating a technological god in its own image.

The suffix "head" refers to the *divine essence* as in "Godhead" (Forasmuch then as we are the offspring of God, we ought not to think that the Godhead is like unto gold, or silver, or stone, graven by art and man's device. Acts 17:29). Machinehead is the replacement of all traditional views of God with the new Living God of the Machine, best illustrated by the recent movie *Transcendence* (2014), which depicts the computer's awaking to consciousness in one mind and will, the Singularity!

Two prophets of modernity plead in a dire warning for us to reconsider modern faith in expansive government and escalating technological acceleration. The first and most notable was master political satirist and critic George Orwell (1903-1950), famous for *Animal Farm* and *1984*, and the second, English literatus Aldous Huxley (1894-1963), author of *Brave New World (BNW)*.

Orwell envisioned the end of history in the all-powerful political dictatorship of *Oceania* marked by perpetual war, omnipresent government surveillance, thought control, and the ubiquitous media projection of Big Brother.

Orwell gave us the foundation of the current age in Cold War politics, but does not serve as guide to the future, which belongs, if humanity allows it, to the apparent benign technophilia of *Brave New World* that follows upon Orwell's cruel political combat boot in the face!

The Cold War Era and *1984*

Orwell divided his fictional geopolitical borders into three grids: *Oceania*, *Eurasia* and *Eastasia*, shadowing accurately Cold War divisions between Western and Eastern Bloc countries allied behind NATO (Oceania) and Warsaw pact nations (Eurasia), leaving the Third World (Eastasia) as pawns (proxy wars) for interminable power battles between the two Super Powers (Super States). Perpetual war characterized normative relations between the superstates in *1984* with the objective to further consolidate the State's power over its own citizens. The threat of war inspires fear in the population and offers government the opportunity and justification for further largesse and control. War insures a permanent state of crisis, leaving the population in desperation for strong leadership and centralized command and control.

The wars of *1984* were a side note to the main thrust of the novel, omnipotent government control. The novel introduced the world to the ominous character Big Brother. The central drama takes place in *Airstrip One*, the capital of *Oceania*, formerly London, England, where Winston Smith the protagonist struggles to maintain his dignity as an individual, under the crushing gears of Fascist government.

Popular criticism asserts that Orwell had Stalinism in the cross hairs in his novel. However, that interpretative ruse acts as an escape clause for the West to disavow any participation in totalitarianism. Most Americans falsely assume that *1984* applied to the Soviet Union and not NATO. Eurasia (the Eastern bloc) was a mere literary foil. Orwell's social criticism applies to all forms of totalitarianism, especially the subtle power structure of the West hidden behind democratic rhetoric, media bias, and an acute lack of national self-criticism. *Oceania* was Orwell's analogy and commentary on the future of the

West after World War II. The NATO alliance, founded in 1949 the same year Orwell published *1984*, was the target of Orwell's criticism and not the Soviet Union.

Brave New World Order in the 21ˢᵗ Century: The Imperial Machine

Huxley's novel *Brave New World* foresaw a techno heaven on earth that knows nothing of wars, political parties, religion or democracy, but caters to creature comforts, maximization of pleasure and minimization of pain; total eradication of all emotional and spiritual suffering through the removal of free choice by radical conditioning from conception in the test tube to blissful euthanasia.

Television was the controlling technology in *1984*, so in *BNW* control is asserted through media, education and a steady flow of *soma*—the perfect drug and chemical replacement for Jesus. "Christianity without tears" was how Mustapha Mond the World Controller described soma. "Anybody can be virtuous now. You can carry at least half your morality around in a [pill] bottle."[48]

Spiritual perfection commanded by Jesus, "Be ye, therefore, perfect, even as your Father, which is in heaven is perfect." (Matthew 5:48, KJV), will be given to all through genetic programming, sustained through chemical infusion and mental conditioning (propaganda). If *1984* was about power for the sake of power, *BNW* emphasizes the kinder, gentler technological dictatorship that does not promise happiness, but delivers it to all whether they want it or Not!

---

[48] Aldous Huxley, *Brave New World* (New York: The Modern Library, 1932), 285.

Brave New World Order amounts to technological totalitarianism, analogous to Huxley's "World State" motto: "Community, Identity, Stability."[49]

The "imperial machine" as it has been called by political scientists acts outside the traditional political process and in tandem with it when needed with no central geographical location or person or groups with any discernable hierarchical structure that directs it; the United States, Great Britain, United Nations, The People's Republic of China or The European Union are not the power brokers of 21st century Empire, but its pawns. Technological Empire rules as an all-encompassing, all-pervasive power, shaping human destiny in its own image.

Transvaluation of Man and Machine

A titanic transvaluation (reversal in the meaning of values) between superstructure (intangible ideological system: beliefs, convictions, morality, myth, etc.) and infrastructure (tangible urban development: roads, buildings, houses, cars, machines, etc.) begun with the Industrial Revolution will finally be complete sometime during the 21st century. Infrastructure replaces superstructure. Technology has become our belief, religion, and hope, what was once a means (technology) to an end (human progress) has replaced the end with the means. Technology replaces humanity as the goal of progress; technology for technology's sake not for the good of mankind or God's glory.

The reversal of meaning is found everywhere in postmodern society beginning with the death of God and unfolding in lock step to the death of man, progress, democracy and Western Civilization; concomitantly

---

[49] Ibid, 1.

paired with an equal ascendancy of all things technological, until the machine ultimately replaces humanity.

Marxist regimes were fond of calling their systems "democratic" or "republic" such as the *People's Republic of China* despite the fact that the *Dictatorship of the Proletariat* bears the opposite meaning. The majestic word *Liberal* once meant freedom from government interference and rule by inner light of reason in the seventeenth century, had come to be synonymous with government regulation and planning by the twentieth century.

The cruelest irony in the transvaluation process is that the triumph of mankind over nature and tradition in the modern world has resulted in his replacement by the machine. Humanism of the modern period promoted the Rational as ideal type of Man. This ideal was already adapted to the machine as *1984* and *Brave New World* illustrated through the removal of faith and the attenuation of human nature to mechanical existence. French Intellectual Jacques Ellul argued further that "This type [of man] exists to support technique [technological acceleration] and serve the machine, but eventually he will be eliminated because he has become superfluous . . . the great hope that began with the notion of human dominance over the machine ends with human replacement by the machine."[50]

The Devil's Logic

What we fear will happen is already here because we fear it; it will overtake us according to our fears; it will recede according to our love. – 1 John 2.

---

[50] Lawrence J. Terlizzese, *Hope in the Thought of Jacques Ellul* (Eugene, OR: Cascade, 104-105).

Human Replacement does not necessarily mean total human extinction, a cyborg race that fundamentally alters human nature will cause a pseudo-extinction— meaning part of humanity, the Machine Class, those most fit for technological evolution will ascend to the next stage, leaving the great majority behind. The movie *Elysium* (2011) offers an excellent illustration: the technological elite, who reap all the benefits from technological advance control the earth from an orbiting space station. H. G. Wells in his famous novel *The Time Machine* painted a similar picture of human evolution that branched into two different species: the hideous cannibalistic Morlocks, "the Under-grounders," their only principle was necessity, feeding off the beautiful, yet docile Eloi, "the Upper-worlders," whose only emotion was fear.[51]

When fear dominates our thinking, love is absent from our motives. To say, "It is necessary" in defense of technological practice, abdicates choice, giving unlimited reign to technological acceleration, i.e. abortion, government surveillance, or digital conversion. "Fear" and "necessity" are the devil's logic. Necessity imposes itself through fear of being left behind by "technological progress."

Necessity is not the Mother of Invention, but the Father of Lies! New technology becomes necessity only after it is invented. There is no conscious need for what does not yet exist. Technological need establishes itself through habitual use creating dependence and finally normalcy in the next generation who cannot relate to a past devoid of modern technological essentials.

"Thy will be done on earth as it is in heaven," serves as our mandate, if we wish to create a future of universal

---

[51] H.G. Wells, *The Time Machine* (New York: Bantam, 1982 [1895]).

love and empathy instead of universal speed and memory.

Knowledge without wisdom leads to disaster. "Where is the wisdom lost in knowledge?"[52] Wisdom is the loving use of knowledge. Love counsels limits to knowledge for the liberation of all. Fear dictates limitless necessity, enslaving all.

A choice faces us. Say "yes!" to God and "no!" to *limitless* advance. Otherwise, mankind faces replacement by the new digital god: Machinehead!

---

[52] Eliot quoted in Huston Smith, *The World's Religions: Our Great Wisdom Traditions* (San Francisco: Harper, 1991, 5).

CHAPTER 4 Human Enhancement and Christianity[53]

Our obsession with perfection and improvement drives the human enhancement movement. But the key is to rest instead in Christ's perfection.

Perfection and Human Enhancement

Americans want to be perfect, and the science of Human Enhancement promises to deliver that ideal. Perfect looks, athletic ability, intelligence, greater productivity, increased longevity and even moral perfectionism are all within reach or so many think. Human Enhancement is the current fashionable term for all the new ways to alter the body and mind to make people fitter and adaptable to the ever-changing pace of progress. Human Enhancement is not an organized school of thought, but a societal-wide trend aimed at achieving perfection. Drugs can be used to enhance an athlete's physical performance in order to perfect his swing or increase a student's intelligence by improving memory and attention span, creating a straight A student. Cosmetic surgeries make women more beautiful and appear younger. The right administration of certain drugs will increase empathy in the brain and help prevent spousal infidelity. Growth hormones given to children make them taller and increase their chances of success. Sex selection is now possible so that you can have the perfect boy/girl balance in your family. Eventually, embryos will be screened to remove undesired genes that lead to obesity or genetic diseases and even determine

---

[53] July 17, 2015

https://www.probe.org/human-enhancement-and-christianity/

hair, skin and eye color. You will be able to custom order the perfect child.

The crux of the Human Enhancement issue surrounds values of perfectionism that desire the technology necessary to make these things possible. Perfection represents a controlling obsession for many Americans. We demand perfect grades from our children. An A- can question an entire academic career. Why not an A? We demand perfection at work. Americans are the hardest workers in history, who have internalized the Protestant Work Ethic like no other people.

And most of all we want perfect bodies that defy age and sickness, epitomizing youth and vitality. Women suffer the hardest under the burden of perfection. Media is saturated with images of young beautiful blonde bodies selling things. Writer Natalia Ilyin asks in her book *Blonde Like Me* the important questions concerning beauty; "Where does our fetish for measurement come from? How do we decide that one person is more good-looking (and therefore 'better') than another? Why do comments made about our fat go to our bone? What happened along the way that made size six beautiful and size twenty a crisis?"[54]

Perfectionism reveals the age-old desire of humanity to aspire to divinity. In the past, we only had myths to follow, but today enhancement technology brings the realization of perfection ever closer.

Apollo as the Old Greek Ideal

We derive our ideals of perfection from historical precedent and desire to master ourselves and the world around us. Our Puritan heritage is one major source for

---

[54] Natalia Ilyin, *Blonde Like Me: The Roots of the Blonde Myth in Our Culture* (New York: Touchstone, 2000), 111.

our obsession with work, thrift, education and industry. Our moral perfectionism has an ancient history we can trace as far back as the fifth-century monk Pelagius, who advocated moral perfection and the power of the will and works righteousness. But our obsession with bodily perfection is even older, and like so many things in the modern world it has its roots in the ancient Greeks. Ilyin notes that "Measurement is the apparatus of mankind's search for perfection. We hear all our lives about the 'perfect body,' 'perfect proportion,' 'perfect features.' But what does perfect mean, really? Where do we get the idea of 'perfect?'"[55]

The Greek philosopher Plato taught that perfection exists in an ideal world outside the everyday one. The perfect apple exists as an idea, and common apples we come into contact with are pale imitations of that ideal. None of the apples we see can compare, but they all derive their nature as apples from the ideal.

Greek religion, too, is still present in striving for perfection. Apollo, the sun god, was believed to embody the perfect human form: young, blond, athletic and male. A beautiful body meant a beautiful mind. "Your blond hair meant that the purity of the sun lived within you. Apollo's blond symbolized the beauty of the power that could order and control nature. It symbolized the beauty of the rational mind."[56] The burden of physical perfection was not always the concern of women but was first located in young men. However, because the Apollo Cult was homoerotic, the image of perfection was transposed to women in Christian times. The beautiful blonde images that consume our culture, such as the blonde on the

---

[55] Ibid.

[56] Ibid., 112.

cover of *Shape* magazine, are really "Apollo in drag," as Ilyin states.[57]

The burden of female perfection reverberates in a recent song by Pink, who sings to her daughter,

Pretty, pretty please
don't you ever ever feel
like you're less than perfect;
pretty, pretty please
if you ever ever feel
like you're nothing,
you are perfect to me.[58]

The ideal of perfection has a way of making us feel like we can never measure up.

Perfection represents an unrealistic goal in any area of life and will always produce the accompanying sense of failure. The desire for divinity as imitation of Apollo or the perfect human form, a striving towards an angelic existence, will always let us down.

Eugenics and Human Enhancement

The goal of Human Enhancement is to improve humanity. This sounds like a noble intention, but as we uncover its meaning, it appears to be fraught with complications. In the past, this was known as *eugenics* or the science of human breeding. Most famously, eugenics is remembered as the basis of Nazi genocide, but it was extremely popular in the United States as well, which served as inspiration and precedent for the Nazi program. Many laws were passed in the 1890's and early 1900's preventing the "feeble-minded," or epileptic,

---

[57] Ibid., 113.

[58] Pink, "Perfect" in Greatest Hits...So Far!!! La Face Records, 2010.

schizophrenic, bi-polar and depressed individuals from marrying and imposing forced sterilization in order to inhibit them from passing on their negative traits.

Eugenics was discredited after the holocaust. Society abandoned it with good cause, yet eugenics is making a comeback. With the advent of biomedical technology, it is now possible to continue the goal of trait selection. Prenatal testing for diseases through the procedure of amniocentesis identifies many complications such as Tay-Sachs, Down Syndrome, sickle-cell anemia, hemophilia, and cystic fibrosis, and also tells the sex of the child. Although prenatal testing can result in early treatment, women may also choose to terminate their pregnancy. This practice has already resulted in an imbalance between male over female children in some regions of India. Ethicists fear the practice will eventually lead to the termination of fetuses believed to carry the genes for obesity, homosexuality, alcoholism and like a ghost from the past, *low intelligence*, even if these genes do not actually exist.[59]

The philosopher Philip Kitcher notes two types of eugenics. The first is known as coercive eugenics and was implemented through state manipulation. Second, he identifies a new kind of eugenics called "laissez-faire eugenics,"[60] also called "liberal eugenics" because it holds the individual choice of trait determination as sovereign. Through sex selection, the perfect boy/girl balance may be achieved along with the elimination of perceived birth defects and genetic flaws, sparing parents the anguish of watching children die slow deaths. However, prenatal testing that leads to trait selection does not resolve the quandary of abortion that is currently necessary to

---

[59] Philip Kitcher, *The Lives to Come: The Genetic Revolution and Human Possibilities* (New York: Tounchstone, 1997), 188.

[60] Ibid., 19.

achieve parental goals. Eugenics is grounded in values and preferences for a certain type of person justified under the rubric of "improvement." The new eugenics offers no opposition to market forces from eventually predetermining any physical characteristic thought most advantageous for success in liberal society, and may return us to the Superman ideal. History teaches the dangers of preoccupation with perfect human form, but people have no ears to hear the lessons of history. We appear destined to repeat the mistakes of the past if we do not change our values that prize strength over weakness or curb our desire for perfection in our children.

Cyborgism

Human Enhancement adopts the cyborg image as its ideal. "Cyborg" was a term coined in 1960 by Manfred Clynes and Nathan Kline, two research scientists wanting to redesign the human body in order to make it adaptable to the inhospitable environment of outer space. It has since come to be applied to the entire human and technological merger. Cyborg is short for *cyber organism*. A cyborg is any living thing that has been adapted to a technological apparatus so that the two are now inseparable. The first animal cyborg was a rat in 1960. It had a Rose osmotic pump attached to its tail which injected chemicals into the body in order to regulate its life support system.[61] Cyborgism is the belief that human adaptation to technology represents the natural development of evolution. Humanity has always used some form of technology, whether fire, knife or arrow, to enhance its existence. The current trend towards our complete absorption into a technological

---

[61] Andy Clark, *Natural-Born Cyborgs: Minds, Technologies, and the Future of Human Intelligence* (New York: Oxford University Press, 2003), 15.

world represents the culmination of a long symbiotic relationship between humanity and its machines. People are, as philosopher Andy Clark says, "Natural-Born Cyborgs."[62] This view argues that we are technological animals, meaning it is human nature to use technology and define ourselves by it.

In her famous essay *A Cyborg Manifesto*, Donna Haraway argues that the Cyborg is the new metaphor or ideal of human existence because it simultaneously transcends and includes all differences.[63]

Both theories argue that the lines of demarcation between humanity, nature and machine are rapidly disappearing. Like a scene out of the movie *Blade Runner* we are rapidly approaching a time where the organic and inorganic worlds will completely merge and the words "natural," "human," and "machine," will no longer mean different things.

This position does not view humanity as either special in some way, or distinct from nature, or possessing a rational soul. It springs from materialism [the worldview that says there is no reality beyond the physical, measurable universe]. Clark argues that this ancient prejudice blinds us from our true technological nature.[64] Clark is right in identifying what Christians call the *imago dei* or image of God as the primary demarcation between humanity and the rest of nature. If this traditional boundary line is lost, the current ideal of "improvement" and "perfection" that leads to a higher evolutionary form can flourish unimpeded.

---

[62] Ibid., 26.

[63] Donna J. Haraway, "A Cyborg Manifesto: Science, Technology, and Socialist-Feminism in the late Twentieth Century" in *Posthumanism*, ed. Neil Badmington (New York: Palgrave, 2000), 69-84.

[64] Clark, *Natural-Born Cyborgs*, 26.

Perfection in Christ

Human Enhancement has restored sight to the blind, brought hearing to the deaf, enabled the lame to walk, and healed diseases—things once thought only possible by miraculous powers. It promises to extend our life expectancy and further increase communication. The realm of possibilities does appear limitless to what new technology will accomplish. However, the ideal of perfection driving our technology is based on an overestimation of human powers and the failure to recognize that our perfection has already been accomplished.

Christians can agree that human beings are technological animals. This is no different than when Aristotle said people are social animals. This just means it is human nature to be social or technological, but we disagree with the notion that we are nothing more than that. Although we were made in the perfect image of God (Gen. 1:26), that image was lost in part due to Adam's sin. We can survive in the harsh conditions of the natural world with technology, which is nothing more than extensions ourselves. But we cannot restore that image without a spiritual rebirth that only God can give us through the work of Christ which we appropriate by faith. Technological enhancement will not lead us to perfection. "Man cannot live by bread alone" (Matt. 4:4, KJV). The Bible calls Jesus Christ the "last Adam" (1 Cor. 15:45) by which it means he was the perfect man sent to restore the human race. "And having been made perfect, He became to all who obey Him the source of eternal salvation" (Heb. 5:10). Humanity constantly strives to recover that lost image through its own good works and religious striving. The technological fetish of our day is simply another form of that works righteousness or humanity trying to earn its own salvation and perfection.

It is the old works righteousness of the Pelagian heresy dressed up in modern garb.

You are called to find your rest in Christ, to accept who you are and not to imitate Apollo (physical form and beauty) or the Cyborg (technology and progress) in reaching for perfection, for they are redeemed in Christ as well. Christ has already accomplished perfection, and we are perfected in Him; "in Him you have been made [perfect] complete" (Col. 2:10). And through Christ, we can extend his example of perfection to the world. "For I am confident of this very thing, that he who began a good work in you will perfect it until the day of Christ Jesus" (Phil. 1:6). Stop striving for a perfect ideal you can never reach. The Psalmist writes, "Be still and know that I am God" (Ps. 46:10, ESV). This is a very difficult task for perfectionists. Our charge is to accept the perfection of Christ, to accept that we have been accepted in Him!

CHAPTER 5 Welcome to the Machine: The Transhumanist God[65]

Authorized Dreams Only Please!

Have you ever wondered if scientists could build a giant machine to solve all the world's problems? Or better yet, why not just become machines and get rid of people all together? Imagine it: no more worries, sickness, war, drug addiction, or poverty. We can solve the world's problems by simply getting rid of people. This sounds fantastic but is actually the goal of the new religion of Transhumanism, which wants to replace the human race with machines.

The wisest man once said there is nothing new under the sun (Ecc. 1:9). Despite all our modern innovation and progress, the age-old desire of mankind to become God remains the same. This new religion is steadily gaining ground, perfectly fit for our hyper-technological twenty-first century. Transhumanism's beliefs are simple, but their implications will be revolutionary. They want to transcend our mortal bodies and create a super intelligent godlike human and machine hybrid, called a cyborg, or something like the Borg from Star Trek. This super machine will solve all our material and spiritual problems by curing disease, extending life expectancy indefinitely, and providing for a meaningful existence through creating a continual sense of euphoria in the brain. There will be no limits to what this superman/machine will be able to do. *All we need to do*

---

[65] January 30, 2012

https://www.probe.org/welcome-to-the-machine-the-transhumanist-god/

is surrender our wills to achieve universal peace and happiness.[66]

Pink Floyd used to sing, "Welcome to the machine. What did you dream? It's alright we told you what to dream."[67] In the brave new world ruled by the cyborg, dreams will all be programmed and peaceful so as not to upset the inhabitants of utopia. With this hybrid technology, someone will make our decisions for us.

All technology expresses its creator's values and represents a certain view of the world, and how things should be. It is anything but value-free. The question for us is, who will decide what the future will be like in a technologically determined age?

You are What You Worship

Technology shapes the human conception of itself and its relation to the world, including our view of God. In a mechanical age, it is not surprising that people

---

[66] Ray Kurzweil, *The Age of Spiritual Machines When Computers Exceed Human Intelligence* (New York:Penguin, 1999); Gregory Stock, *Metaman:The Merging of Humans and Machines into a Global Superorganism* (New York: Simon and Schuster, 1993); Lewis Mumford, *The Transformations of Man* (New York: Collier, 1956); Jacques Ellul, *The Technological Society*, (New York: Vintage, 1964), 428-436. It was techno critics like Ellul and Mumford that saw the techno future more clearly and soberly than the previously noted Transhumanists. Ellul argued that information would eventually pass from the machine straight to the human brain electronically without being processed through consciousness and that breeding will all be done through artificial means, and natural procreation will be forbidden (432, 433). Whatever problems and disturbances the technology of the future will create will be solved through "a world-wide totalitarian dictatorship" (434). This is exactly what Transhumanist philosophy will bring. Mumford argued that modern technical society will eventually produce a machine replacement for man (*The Transformations of Man*, 100, 117-132).

[67] Pink Floyd, "Welcome to the Machine" in *Wish You Were Here*, Capitol, 1975.

conceive of themselves and others as machines.[68] Human relationships are reduced to efficiency and usefulness or to convenient arrangements. For example, marriage is already largely viewed as an economic contract between two people who may not have anything else in common, rather than as a sacrificial commitment.

Transhumanist philosophy takes the modern mechanistic view to its ultimate level of altering humanity to become a machine. The idea that we become the thing we worship finds the greatest expression in the twenty-first century. Those who worship idols become like them (Ps. 115). Those who worship money become greedy. Those who worship drugs become addicted, and those who worship the machine will become a machine. In the past, philosophers and poets often used the machine as a metaphor of dehumanization and alienation from modern life; modern society was thought to function like a machine.[69] This means in a machine culture, people feel like numbers or spare parts and therefore entirely expendable. Individual meaninglessness in a mechanistic society will be realized in the very near future so that individuals will be spare parts and completely assimilated. The future supercomputer will offer humanity everything, except the freedom not to choose assimilation.

The machine represents the ideal existence, even the ideal being. The idea of "salvation in the machine" derives from modern thought in a deistic and Unitarian

---

[68] Cecelia Tichi, *Shifting Gears: Technology, Literature, Culture in Modernist America* (Chapel Hill, NC: The University of North Carolina Press, 1987), 16; David F. Noble, *The Religion of Technology: The Divinity of Man and the Spirit of Invention* (New York: Knopf, 1997), 143-171.

[69] Karl Jaspers, *Man in the Modern Age* (New York: Anchor Books, 1951); Nicols Fox, Against the Machine: The Hidden Luddite Tradition in Literature, Art and Individual Lives (Washington DC: Island Press, 2002).

God who created a clockwork universe.[70] Transhumanism has simply transposed that deity into the machine itself and removed the Clock Maker. Now it's the clock they worship.

Transhumanism affirms artificial selection instead of natural selection. They believe that through science and technology, humanity can direct the cause of evolution. Humanity controls its own evolutionary process to reach a perfectible state. Instead of millions of years to evolve a new species, it will be done in decades, maybe even in one generation.

The Singularity Is Near

Transhumanists expect the merger of humanity and machine around 2045 in an event they call the Singularity. This means artificial intelligence (AI) will equal or exceed human intelligence, and there will no longer be any discernible difference. Humanity will lose all distinct consciousness and consider itself as one being.[71]

Humanity then must change itself genetically to keep pace with AI. This will create a giant planetary super organism that knows no distinctions. Humanity will merge with the rest of nature through genetic engineering, and nature will become indistinguishable from the machine. We will no longer know the difference between organic and inorganic, or natural and artificial, something already prevalent today in cities, weather patterns, and food production.

---

[70] Lewis Mumford, *The Myth of the Machine: The Pentagon of Power* (New York: Harvest, 1970), 33; Noble, *The Religion of Technology*, 146; Mary Midgley, *Science as Salvation: A Modern Myth and Its Meaning* (New York: Routledge, 1992).

[71] Lev Grossman, "2045: The Year Man Becomes Immortal", *Time* (February 21, 2011), 43-49.

A super organism looks something like a beehive, anthill, or termite mound; various individual cells work together as one. So by mid-century Transhumanism envisions total global unity, not at the political level between states, but ontologically and biologically. We will have evolved into one massive planet—truly Spaceship Earth, completely interrelated and interdependent, like an anthill. This will be the technological version of the kingdom of God or the Transhumanist version of the millennium.

Ray Kurzweil and the Singularitarians believe people will eventually be able to upload their consciousness into a computer and live forever. [Note: for an intriguing Christian perspective on this idea in a compelling novel, Probe recommends *The Last Christian* by David Gregory.] The religious nature of this movement is obvious in its millennialism or belief in the coming perfect society, and also in its belief in progress and immortality. Critics call the Singularity "the rapture of the nerds," indicating its close connection with religious belief and millennial expectations. The Singularity represents religious belief for computer geeks. The acceptance of progress and human perfection makes Transhumanism the heir of modernity, with its ideal of technological utopianism and its mechanistic view of the body. It's modernism with a vengeance.

The Artilect War

The future may not bring the perfection of the Singularity, but the disaster of the Artilect War. An Artilect is an artificial intelligence or super computer. AI researcher Hugo de Garis predicts that the Transhumanist vision will be disastrous and will result in gigadeath (the death of billions of people). He hypothesizes that by the end of the century, Cosmists, or technically modified people, will want to build Artilects to join with humanity, but that Terrans, or unmodified people, will oppose their construction because it has no benefit to them. A nuclear war will ensue, probably initiated by Terrans as their only way to stop Cosmists.[72]

Jacques Ellul once remarked that "the technical society must perfect the 'man-machine' complex or risk total collapse."[73] There is no other place to go but up. If the current human enhancement project fails it may prove to have devastating effects for the future of the human race, and if it succeeds the human race faces techno-enslavement or pseudo-extinction by being transformed into another species.

Will the Singularity really happen? It is very possible. Or maybe the Artilect War will happen instead. Perhaps technology will bring the apocalypse instead of utopia. It is all science fiction right now, but science fiction is often correct in the broadest terms. Recall Jules Verne's vision of space travel to the moon in the nineteenth century when people thought it was pure fantasy and laughed because there was no way to break earth's gravitational pull. But his work inspired a generation of rocket scientists to find a way to do it, and within a century man was walking on the moon. Something considered impossible was achieved.[74]

A basic principle of futurism states that anything is possible to achieve within twenty years given the resources to do it. And the Bible states that nothing is impossible for humanity in a unified technological

---

[72] Hugo De Garis, *The Artilect War: Cosmists vs. Terrans: A Bitter Controversy Concerning Whether Humanity Should Build Godlike Massively Intelligent Machines* (Palm Springs, CA: Etc Publications, 2005).

[73] Ellul, *The Technological Society*, 414.

[74] Howard E. McCurdy, *Space and the American Imagination* (Washington DC: Smithsonian Institute Press, 1997), 9-27.

society. Gen. 11:6 says "Now nothing that they imagined will be impossible for them." This, of course, is talking about Babel, but I think it demonstrates the fact that the discussion of a transhuman transformation should be taken as a credible threat and should be addressed by the church.

Ethic of Limits

The essence of Transhumanist philosophy revolves around the idea that there are no natural or divine limits to what technology can accomplish. It serves the basic technological imperative that says what can be done should be done! This view unleashes all restraint and frees us from all limits, and is one of the greatest examples of the church's cultural captivity since we do not present a different view of technology from the rest of society.

This maxim is obviously dangerous because any limitless action leads to self-destruction as a natural corrective. Humanity cannot presume to be greater than the natural limits arrayed against it, such as death or the scarcity of resources. Humanity must learn to live within boundaries.

Christians are called to respect limits and the right balance in its use of technology, between its misuse and its non-use. In an age of limitless technology, the church must present an ethic of limitation. This means finding limits to technology, such as limiting computer use, limiting driving, electricity, or even not upgrading. This may seem small, but in trying to discover a workable ethic of technology, it represents something we can do right now. The widow's mite (Mark 12:41-43) will not solve the church's budget deficit, but should be given anyway because it was something she could do, so an ethic of limitation remains a course of action open.

An ethic of limitation only becomes obvious when the situation appears desperate, such as with nuclear weapons, where not even one mishap can be afforded. Other examples consist of overeating, drug addiction, over-fishing or hunting, or any activity that exhausts natural resources. Because people did not practice limits, to begin with, they are now faced with a real possibility of collapse or catastrophe. We must discover the limits to any technology if we are to use technology correctly and benefit from it. The history of the Tower of Babel teaches that if mankind does not practice self-control, God will impose limits Himself in judgment. – Genesis 11:1-9.

CHAPTER 6 The Church and the Social Media Revolution[75]

Dr. Lawrence Terlizzese examines social media's massive communication shift, with insights for the church.

What is Social Media?

Any media that uses two-way communication as opposed to one-way communication is *social media* rather than *mass media*, such as TV, radio, and print which deliver a message to a mass audience. Mass media is not personal like the telephone or letter writing; it is directed to the crowd or to a particular niche in the crowd that does not allow for the audience to talk back, with some exceptions. Mass media is not social because it does not permit a conversation with its audience. Social media, such as social websites like Facebook, Twitter, and the new Youtoo Social TV website, allows for dialogue and two-way communication between speaker and audience. It is dialogue rather than monologue. Social media use is not limited to just the popular websites. Any form of electronic communication involving computers and cell phones is part of the social media revolution because these technologies offer the individual the ability to respond.

It is estimated that one-third of the world is now connected to the internet. If you have an email address, you are involved in social media. This sizeable amount constitutes a revolution in communication because it changes the *way* we communicate and it changes *what* we communicate. In calling social media a revolution we

---

[75] June 16, 2015

https://www.probe.org/the-church-and-the-social-media-revolution/

simply mean this is a new way of communicating. It does not mean mass media will be abolished. Media, along with most technological progress, operates in a layering system where a new layer or technology builds on the old one rather than abolishing it. Mass media begins with the printing press. The telephone, radio and TV come later. Television remains the most prominent mass medium; while the printed word has not disappeared, it is certainly not as central as it was in the nineteenth century. The computer adds another layer to our media and brings them all together. It will overshadow them all, but not abolish them.

With about a third of the actual world online or engaged in social media, it is necessary that the church, which is in the business of communication, makes sure its message is accurately represented there. But the task is not as easy as starting a new profile page since there are certain problems that must be addressed as we communicate.

The Medium Is the Message

Close to 2,247,000,000 people use social media worldwide. This is a remarkable change in just a few years and easily qualifies as a new way of communicating, unprecedented in the history of the world. It is a revolution because it changes the way we communicate from individual face-to-face contact to an electronic mediation with certain advantages and disadvantages.

We have all heard the saying, "the medium is the message."[76] This means the way we say something is as important as what we say, or that the medium affects the

---

[76] Marshall McLuhan, *Understanding Media: The Extensions of Man* (New York: McGraw Hill, 1964).

content of what is said. Preaching is not unaffected by this principle. Simply because someone preaches the word of God does not mean immunity to the potential negative aspects of his chosen medium just as with radio, TV, and the internet. For example, radio and TV are effective in reaching a mass audience, but this usually must come at the expense of the quality of the message; it must be toned down to fit these media. Any subject with many ideas and complex logic may work in a book format but not on TV. Telephones put you in touch with a disembodied voice, superior to not talking or letter writing, but still not as good as actually talking to someone in person. Anyone involved with persuasion in business deals where you absolutely must communicate a convincing point knows the importance of body language, tone of voice, eye contact, appearance, and attitude—all conveyed by personal presence but lost over the phone. The phone itself shapes what you say by how it is said. It reduces communication from all five senses to one: hearing. The results are predictable: the phone reduces communication compared to actually being there.

A basic law of media says the wider the audience, the less substantive a message simply because it must appeal to the common denominator in the general audience. The more people you want to reach, the less of a message you will have, which means keep it simple when it comes to a general audience so the majority of people can understand it. This is the drawback of instant and mass communication. We sacrifice quality of thought and depth of analysis for instant access to a mass audience and for immediate applicability of a general principle. In other words, we are telling people what to do without reflection, which is time-consuming, slow, and simply awkward. Analysis is meant for the personal level, and mass communication is not personal. The reductionist trend in media can be circumvented to some extent through niche audiences which many social media sites actually represent. This is a fair reflection of actual communities. What is society but the collection of smaller groups put into a whole?

Disembodiment

Social media represents a disembodied form of community. This, of course, is the nature of long distance relationships and communication. The reduction of knowledge to its simplest forms brings with it the sense that knowledge or community is simply information. The gospel can be communicated as information, but it is more than that. The same is true with traditional forms of preaching, books, or even TV. We know after all has been said there still remains a side of the gospel that must be experienced or encountered in real people. The gospel must be embodied and not simply read about or talked about. This was the gist of Paul's exhortation to the Corinthians: "you are a letter of Christ . . . written not with ink, but with the Spirit of the living God, not on tablets of stone, but on tablets of human hearts" (2 Cor. 3:3-4). We might as well say written not electronically on the transient screen with flickering pixels, but in flesh and blood and in one-to-one encounters with friends, family, and neighbors. Media, as good as it is, cannot substitute for the personal experience of God and fellowship with others. This brings the idea of an online community, church or school into question. There is no doubt that people communicate this way effectively, even on Facebook, and they can learn through this medium just like any traditional means, but there is a doubt as to how qualitative one's learning or one's community will be if there is no personal encounter. Can long lasting bonds and relationships form strictly through electronic means?

Social media is excellent at giving you a wide audience just like TV and radio and even meeting new people, but it is not a replacement for face-to-face contact. Media technology may best be seen as an excellent supplement to relationships and community, but not a replacement. It can be used to stay in touch and keep people connected, but in cannot ultimately replace our community and social network of actual people. I think the goal of an online church should be to get people out from behind a computer and into contact and fellowship with others. Social media can facilitate friendship, but it cannot replace it. We are warm-blooded creatures and need other warm-blooded people to have a community, something a computer screen cannot provide. Social media serves as a supplement to the community, not a substitute!

Social Media and Privacy

What happens in Vegas stays on YouTube, Facebook, and Twitter. Privacy is dead. The computer killed it, and no one cares. Every step forward in technological progress has a price to pay. We have moved forward in creating social media, which enables us to communicate with a wider audience, but society has paid a terrible price with the loss of privacy. The computer remembers everything. This reality should cause some pause and reflection on what we say simply because it can be potentially recalled and even used against us. Employers routinely check Facebook pages of potential employees. Creditors use Facebook to collect debts. The police use Facebook to find people and build cases against them. We think of social media as fun and games, much like a video game, when in fact it is much more serious. All social media communication such as email or texting exists in a nether world between an illusion of privacy and the potential public access by everyone. The user falsely assumes his message is private without realizing it may be available to anyone. Future generations will archive and access all that we say today.

Even more seriously, the NSA is currently building a supercomputer called the Utah Data Center scheduled to go online in 2013 that will monitor all your digital actions including email, cell phone calls, even Google searches.[77] It will be able to track all your purchases electronically. Whatever you do digitally will be available for scrutiny by the government. I know you wanted to hear how great social media is for communicating, evangelism, and so forth, and it is great, but there are pitfalls and dangers that we must also confront. Let's not get so swept up in our enthusiasm for social media that we stick our head in the sand when it comes to the dangers. This is the greatest problem I see Christians make when they analyze technology. They see only the advantages and positive sides of their technological involvement and refuse to consider what may go wrong. It will not create a damper to analyze the potential problems of our technology use; rather it will make us sober-minded as we are commanded to be (1 Peter 1:13, 4:7 and 5:8).

Dialogue vs. Monologue

Social media does offer a great advantage over the traditional means of mass communication that the church has used in print, TV, and radio. Social media represents a democratization of media including TV. Mass media is traditionally one-sided communication or monologue where one powerful voice does all the speaking, especially on TV. Social media allows for multiple voices to be heard at once and in contrast with each other, allowing for a dialogue and conversation as opposed to

---

[77] James Bamford, "The NSA is Building the Country's Biggest Spy Center (watch what you say)" in *Wired* March 17, 2012.

the pedagogy of monologue. This is significant because, as we are told by media experts like Marshall McLuhan and Jacques Ellul, propaganda is usually the result of only one voice being permitted in a discussion or the absence of dialogue, much like in a commercial where only one viewpoint is promoted. McLuhan notes the importance of dialogue with media: "The environment as a processor of information is propaganda. Propaganda ends where dialogue begins. You must talk to the media, not to the programmer. To talk to the programmer is like complaining to a hot dog vendor at a ballpark about how badly your favorite team is playing."[78]

Really, for the first time in history does the general public have a chance to talk back to knowledge brokers and those creating information and to those creating faith. A few tell the many what to think through mass media; through social media, an individual tells the mass what he thinks. Social media offers a multitude of voices on all topics. It may appear chaotic and directionless at times, and at other times there appears incisive wisdom. Social media reflects the turmoil and sanity of its users. Social media is many things, but unlike its big brother mass media, social media is not propaganda. The church needs to join this conversation soberly.

---

[78] Marshall McLuhan and Quentin Fiore, *The Medium is the Message: An Inventory of Effects* (New York: Bantam, 1967, 142); Jacques Ellul, *Propaganda: The Formation of Men's Attitudes* (New York: Vintage, 1965).

CHAPTER 7 2012: Doomsday All Over Again[79]

Progress or Regress

It is the end of the world again. The world was predicted to end at least eight times in the past 30 years, from the Jupiter Effect in 1982 to what became a common punch line, "88 reasons why the rapture will happen in 1988." Then there was the granddaddy of all false apocalyptic prophecies: the millennium bug of 2000 when it was widely held that all computers would fail at the turn of the millennium. Let's not forget the two failed predictions of the end in 2011. Now the world faces yet another prediction of the end with the Mayan calendar prophecy of 2012. In an age of super–science, computers, space travel and accelerating progress, why are people fascinated with the end of the world?

We have all heard the phrase "What goes up must come down." This captures the popular attitude towards progress and regress. Americans believe strongly in human perfectibility and the inevitability of technological progress. This idea states that as technology moves society from its primitive state to an advanced condition, it will eventually improve, bringing a better tomorrow. The world is getting better and better. Faith in progress provides the engine for all the accelerating technological changes from space exploration, media, computers, to science and medicine. Historian Robert Nisbet noted the essential role of progress in our belief system when he said that progress does not represent one aspect of modern life, but in fact provides the keystone idea and

---

[79] January 5, 2012

https://www.probe.org/2012-doomsday-all-over-again/

context for the entire modern worldview, including democracy, equality, social justice and, of course, science and technology.[80] The modern world does not exist without the belief in progress. Technological improvement makes no sense without the larger *telos*, or purpose of history, guiding it. Simply put, all of this innovation leads to a utopian future.

So we are left with the question If America is so progressive why is it so obsessed with the end of the world or apocalypticism, a belief that is not progressive, but regressive? This view of history does not move toward a utopian society of universal peace, ease, and convenience, but rather toward calamity. Progress and regress share the same view of history. Any belief in progress necessarily has a regressive interpretation. They each look at the same circumstances and data and draw complementary conclusions. One sees the dawn of a great society; the other sees the end of the world. They represent complementary ideas in the same way life and death complements each other. What lives eventually dies, so what progresses will also necessarily regress.

All people intuitively know that they will die one day; so then, society, the collective "person," knows it too must one day die. If progress takes place, we know that its opposite, regress, will also happen. Regressive thought states that the progress we take for granted potentially has a downside and in fact will result in something catastrophic. Our society will one day come to an end. It cannot live forever any more than an individual can live forever in a mortal body. We know that what goes up must come down. The current obsession with the end of the world in movies, such as *2012*, *Melancholia* and *Contagion* or wildly popular novels such as the *Left Behind* series, the predictions of

---

[80] Robert Nisbet, History of the Idea of Progress (New York: Basic Books, 1980), 9, 171.

popular preachers or the Mayan prophecy all cater to our regressive and pessimistic side. This is not as bad as it first sounds. Death creates the foundation of all religion, philosophy and culture as attempts to provide answers for our questions and solace in times of doubt and need. The reality of death causes people to look for the meaning of life. Christians need to harness the regressive side of culture because it warns of imminent danger and offers the opportunity to introduce people to Jesus Christ. Regressive thinking, like the knowledge of our own death, makes us all aware of our need for God and the Savior. Believers must take advantage of this primal consciousness of the end to tell people about what the Bible says concerning the end of the world and the return of Christ. But in order to do this successfully, we must first establish guidelines on how to identify false prophecy.

What the Bible Says

Today people are searching for the meaning of life in the wrong places, such as the prophecies of Nostradamus, astrology and, again, the Mayan prophecy of 2012. It is a sign of the end times when there are many false prophets talking about the end of the world (Matt. 24:11). The false prophet shows that people are aware that the end is near.

There are two rules in Scripture that will help believers identify false prophets, which should be followed without exception. First, *prophecy must never set a date regarding when the world will end.* Jesus spoke clearly about the signs of His return and the end of the world when He said, "But of that day and hour no one knows" (Matt. 24:36).[81] Anyone who comes to you with

---

[81] Christian Publishing House (January 01, 2016)

a firm date as to when the world will end such as December 21, 2012, should be avoided. Cultists continually violate this cardinal rule. For example, the Jehovah's Witnesses have predicted the end of the world eight times between 1914 and 1975. Popular radio preacher Harold Camping predicted the end in 1994 and twice in 2011. The speculation surrounding the year 2000 was much like it is today over 2012. Scientific evidence was proffered predicting that all computers would fail at the turn of the last millennium. This warning was taken very seriously by most people who made preparations for the potential disaster, demonstrating the pervasive sentiment of impending doom.

However, many Bible-believing Christians also fall prey to the error of date setting, even if this practice is often veiled in vague language and logic. For example, when prophecy experts identify leading political figures as the Antichrist, such as Hitler, Mussolini or Saddam Hussein, they engage in false prophecy. This approach will invariably get us into trouble because it starts the clock ticking. If Saddam Hussein were the Antichrist, then logically Christ should have returned before the end of his life, since the Antichrist is the precursor to the coming of Christ. (Rev. 6:2; 2 Thess. 2:3) However, we know that did not happen. In this way, identification of the Antichrist with any leading figure becomes false prophecy.

How much better it would have been to say *Hussein was like the Antichrist* or prefigured the Antichrist, rather than identify him as the Antichrist. This simple switch in focus spares us the humiliation of false prophecy but retains all the power of moral denunciation that apocalyptic thinking offers.

The SECOND COMING of CHRIST: Basic Bible Doctrines of the Christian Faith by Edward D. Andrews (ISBN-13: 978-0692611135)

This leads to the second rule of identifying false prophecy: all prophecy must have a *moral imperative*. This means people should not engage in speculation and prognostication for the fun of it. A biblical approach to prophecy gives a warning about future judgment and a chance to repent, "Blessed is he who reads and those who hear the words of the prophecy, and heed the things which are written in it; for the time is near" (Rev. 1:3; see also 2 Thess. 2:1, 5-10). Prophecy engages in denouncing moral outrage, which is why it couches things in the strongest possible language. To say that the world is coming to an end or that someone is the Antichrist gets a lot of attention, but requires a moral cause to justify its claims.

If the prophecy gives a date and it lacks the moral imperative, then the prophecy reveals itself to be false and sensationalistic. The Mayan 2012 prophecy fails on both counts. Although it causes us to contemplate the end, it sets a date and offers no reason for why the world should end. It is simply doomsday all over again!

CHAPTER 8 "Why Does God Allow Natural Evils Such as Tsunamis, Hurricanes, and Earthquakes?"[82]

My question is about natural evils such as tsunamis, hurricanes, earthquakes, etc. I feel like the problem of moral evil such as murder and stealing is solved by the free will defense, but I haven't heard a good refutation of why God allows tsunamis and other natural events to take out huge villages and kill children.

The so-called "natural evils" such as natural disasters are only evil from a human perspective. Tsunamis and earthquakes are normal and necessary occurrences in nature. We could not live on planet earth without them. They shape the environment and contribute to an inhabitable planet. They are part of a normal cycle of nature, along with every other occurrence in nature such as volcanoes, floods and even disease and plague, which is God's way of maintaining balance in the ecology, necessary for human survival. These natural occurrences only become evil when humanity gets in their way. This sometimes has to do with human choices and "moral evil." For example building huge population centers on known fault lines and danger zones and not taking proper precautions in construction or having an efficient evacuation plan and warning system in place. Humanity cannot do away with the normal cycles of nature because we need a healthy natural environment to live. But we can adjust ourselves to nature in order to mitigate some

---

[82] February 26, 2013

https://www.probe.org/why-does-god-allow-natural-evils-such-as-tsunamis-hurricanes-and-earthquakes/

of its more deadly effects on civilization. New Orleans is the perfect example of human arrogance, neglect, and apathy in the face of known dangers from hurricanes. This city did not take the proper precautions in building a technological defense against hurricanes when it was known for decades that it was in danger of a disaster. The Netherlands is an example of a country that did take the proper precautions in protecting itself from flooding and goes on to survive without incident. So should we blame God for the apathy of New Orleans? This means there is not a strict separation between natural and moral evil and that they are more interwoven than we realize or care to admit.

Now, many times natural disasters are not the result of human choices. We have two options. First, it is a judgment of God. Second, we don't know why, other than saying God has a purpose in this disaster that we don't understand, which is certainly an acceptable choice; that is how the problem of evil is explained in the book of Job. I am not averse to saying natural disasters are a judgment from God. The Bible has no problem calling natural disasters judgments—floods and earthquakes are perfect examples. This does not mean that every natural disaster is a judgment. I am only saying judgment is a possibility.

Therefore, there are three possible answers to your question. Natural disasters happen as a result of human choices. They are a judgment of God or they happen for a reason we do not understand.

Feel free to follow up on any of these issues with me if you like. – Lawrence Terlizzese, Ph.D.[83]

---

[83] Christian Publishing House (March 24, 2015)

IF GOD IS GOOD Why Does God Allow Suffering? By Edward D. Andrews (ISBN-13: 978-0692414620)

Epilogue

Jacques Ellul described the promise of technology to create a better world than the one inherited from nature and tradition a gigantic bluff; "There is a bluff here because the effective possibilities are multiplied a hundredfold . . . and the negative aspects are radically concealed."[84] The wager of technology was that *la technique* will be able to replace earth's natural environment with a technological one that will prove better.

Technological innovation is embraced without question, evaluation or moral scrutiny, without concern for the potential risks, costs, and inevitable side effects that accompanies new technology. Technology "is regarded in advanced as the only solution to collective problems," such as war, pollution unemployment and personal problems, health, family, "even the meaning of life," [85] and is presented as the world's only hope for progress. Thus creating a world full of diversion and illusion, jettisoning normal concerns and fears over new technology leaving humanity vulnerable to technology's failure and deceived by false promises that technological progress will create a better world tomorrow than the one we have today.

I would add that this technological bluff is a lie and clever front concealing a pernicious deception. A subtle theft and subsequent destruction of human heritage is being perpetrated by the purveyors of a technological future no one asked for devoid of nature and tradition.

---

http://www.christianpublishers.org/apps/webstore/products/show/5786449

[84] Jacques Ellul, *The Technological Bluff*, trans., by Geoffrey W. Bromiley (Grand Rapids: Eerdmans, 1990), xvi.

[85] Ibid.

Human heritage taken for granted in every generation past will not be in our digital future. Like Jacob swindling a famished and beleaguered Esau out of his birth rite for food, or the Manhattan tribe selling their ancestral island to the Dutch for twenty-four dollars in beads, so technological progress kills off nature, cultural differences, depth and complexity of thought and religious belief. It should come as no surprise to readers that the social forces creating the technological future they may hold so dear are the same that killed God in the 20th century. And is no friend to mankind.

In exchange for eternal imprisonment in the Omnipticon, humanity must give up the freedom and blessed diverse abundance of the natural world, and must surrender personal identity, tradition, belief or conviction, all that separates and confirms a unique personality, the right to privacy. People will no longer be identified by name, but numbers and their separate group affinities, such as churches, families, local communities, regional distinction such as North and South will soon dissolve into a hive mentality. It is impossible to calculate the spiritual heritage lost in vanishing open spaces, starry nights, encounters with wild beasts, the forest, the campfire; or witnessing the stampede as in *Dances with Wolves*, 1990; in their stead we get 500 channels on cable TV now, and the average lifespan will soon reach 100 years.

Development, suburban sprawl, pollution, overfishing, roads, highways, automobiles, deforestation, overpopulation, etc., are destroying the Green Earth and will ultimately create a desert planet. Earth loses 30,000 species of plants and animals a year out of an estimated 10 million total as a direct result of the expansion of modern technological infrastructure–the city. How many cures for terminable diseases have been lost in the ecocide?

Urbanization and desertification of the planet are complimentary effects of technological progress since the industrial revolution. The logical result, *if we let it happen*, will look something like the science fiction of Judge Dredd, earth reduced to a desert world through industrialization and war, inhabited by one totalitarian industrial Mega City. Even if Dr. Will Caster (Johnny Depp) did transcend and become an Artilect (god-like supercomputer) as in the movie *Transcendence* (2014), the Artilect will not be able to reverse the loss of natural resources, and limitation of space, the hypothetical use (hope) of nanotechnology, microscopic helper robots imitating and restructuring nature will not be able to replace nature either nor restore what is currently being lost.

However, it is entirely predictable how an Artilect probably not unlike Colossus (*Colossus: The Forbin Project*, 1970) will resolve overpopulation and resource depletion, given the current trend in following computer projections or modeling, the world government will comply, or Colossus will force them to capitulate. Having no feelings or empathy or even moral restraint, good or bad, love or fear, righteous or immoral does not compute. The decision-making process of the computer post-Singularity will be no different than today or when it was first invented "yes/no", it'll just be faster with chic Hollywood voices for dramatic effect. In a crisis of overpopulation, resource sacristy, the Transcendent will convey on the world the gift of food like manna from heaven, except it will be more like Soylent Green instead. Why would a computer not suggest cannibalism between human beings if that were the most efficient way to reduce earth's surplus population? On what moral basis will anyone object to the technological innovation of New World Manna feeding the planet? Hive mind does not know how to object it only obeys.

In the famous cinematic ending, "Soylent Green is people!" (*Soylent Green*, 1973) lurks the *pernicious deception* of the technological bluff, the false promise of technology. Call the bluff! How so? Just cut the cord! Technological progress operates as all Leviathans do according to an inner causal deterministic logic (cause and effect), or the law of self-preservation and promotion. When left to its own devices Leviathan will be true to nature and devour everything, then self-destruct. However, if the future result or effect is already known on the basis of causal logic and historical precedent, then the outcome can be changed through *reversal of cause*. Professor Capaldi noted that "If we know the necessary conditions of an event then we can *prevent* it from happening. Remove any necessary condition, and the effect does not take place." [86] There will be no perfection of technological singularity where a voice of dissent is heard coupled with the practice of slow regression away from its completion. Total system control will not be effective where differences of opinion are radically maintained. If however, the voice of conscientious objection, the thorn in the flesh of all absolute systems is silenced then the Singularity will encircle us that is the point of no return!

As to the problem or inability to "unplug" from the system the solution is very simple, unplug, disconnect, turn off, cut the cord; in other words, practice a code of limited use of technology as much as possible, especially at the point of technological convergence in the microcomputer (cell phone, smartphone) or microcomputer chip, now before the point of no return and technological addiction warps the will to freedom and difference. Technological oblivion, nirvana, black out

---

[86] Nicholas Capaldi and Miles Smit, *The Art of Deception: An Introduction to Critical* Thinking (Amherst: New York: Prometheus Books, 2007), 197.

or Singularity is the most pervasive threat to human freedom, dignity, and survival but the easiest to defeat by pressing the off button. I suggest personal small regressive steps backward away from techno-abyss until collectively reaching manageable use or societal equilibrium between effective uses of technology, sustainable resources, and freedom not to use any given technology on the basis of conscience or faith. The 1960's Hippie mantra, "tune in, turn on and drop out" needs some rewording for the 21st-century struggle for freedom, I propose simply, "turn off, press off, and switch off!" And if all else fails, just cut the cord!

Shinedown sings in their music video "Cut the Cord" a hymn to freedom's victory from all addiction that shouts back into the abyss with thundering cannonade of light and sound, never departing from the path of total victory that begins with the smallest steps of faith the size of a mustard seed capable of moving mountains and accomplishing the impossible (Matthew 17: 20 and Luke 17: 6); "Freedom, follow me . . . cut it . . . Now victory is all you need, So cultivate and plant the seed, Hold your breath and count to ten, just count to ten ... cut the cord, Freedom . . . You gotta feel courage, Embrace possession, If it was easier to shatter everything that ever mattered, But it's not, because it's your obsession, Be a fighter, backbone, desire, Complicated and it stings, (but we both know what it means), And it's time to get real and inspired . . . Don't be a casualty, cut the cord, cut the cord." [87]

At this moment of our history, the one best way forward is to go backward, to regress is to progress, turn off the power in order to see the light!

---

[87] Shinedown, "Cut the Cord" *Threat to Survival* (Atlantic, 2015).

Bibliography

Benz, Ernst. *Evolution and Christian Hope: Man's Concept of the Future from Early Fathers to Teilhard de Chardin trans.*, Heinz G. Frank. New York: Doubleday, 1966.

Bourne, Jr., Joel K. *The End of Plenty: The Race to feed A Crowed World.* New York: Norton, 2015.

Clark, Andy. *Natural-Born Cyborgs: Minds, Technologies, and the Future of Human Intelligence.* New York: Oxford University Press, 2003.

Ellul, Jacques. *"New Hope for the Technological Society: An Interview with Jacques Ellul" in.* Et cetera 40.2, 1983.

—. *Propaganda: The Formation of Men's Attitudes.* New York: Vintage, 1965.

—. *The Technological Society.* New York: Vintage, 1964.

—. *The Technological System, trans., by Joachim Neugroschel.* New York: Continuum, 1980.

Floyd, Pink. *"Welcome to the Machine" in Wish You Were Here.* Los Angeles: Capitol Records, 1975.

Fox, Nicols. *Against the Machine: The Hidden Luddite Tradition in Literature, Art and Individual Lives.* Washington DC: Island Press, 2002.

Garis, Hugo De. *The Artilect War: Cosmists vs. Terrans: A Bitter Controversy Concerning Whether Humanity Should Build Godlike Massively Intelligent Machines.* Palm Springs, CA: Etc Publications, 2005.

Gregory, David. *The Last Christian.* Colorado Springs: Waterbrook Press, 2010.

Grossman, Lev. "2045: The Year Man Becomes Immortal ." *Tme*, February 21, 2011: 43-49.

Haraway, Donna J. *"A Cyborg Manifesto: Science, Technology, and Socialist-Feminism in the late Twentieth Century"* in *Posthumanism*, ed. Neil Badmington. New York: Palgrave, 2000.

Heidegger, Martin. *"The Question Concerning Technology"* in *The Question Concerning Technology and Other Essays*, trans. by William Lovitt. New York: Harper, 1977.

Huxley, Aldous. *Brave New World*. (New York: The Modern Library, 1932.

Ilyin, Natalia. *Blonde Like Me: The Roots of the Blonde Myth in Our Culture*. New York: Touchstone, 2000.

Jaspers, Karl. *Man in the Modern Age*. New York: Anchor Books, 1951.

—. *Man in the Modern Age*, trans., by Eden and Cedar Paul. New York: Anchor Books, 1957.

Jünger, Friedrich Georg. *The Failure of Technology*. New York: Gateway, 1949.

Kitcher, Philip. *The Lives to Come: The Genetic Revolution and Human Possibilities*. New York: Tounchstone, 1997.

Kurzweil, Ray. *The Age of Spiritual Machines When Computers Exceed Human Intelligence*. New York: Penguin, 1999.

—. *The Singularity is Near*. New York: Penguin, 2005.

Lewis, C. S. *The Abolition of Man*. New York: Macmillan, 1947.

Malthus, Thomas R. *An Essay on the Principle of Population.* Amherst, NY: Prometheus Books, 1998.

McCurdy, Howard E. "Space and the American Imagination." *Smithsonian Institute Press*, 1997: 9-27.

McLuhan, Marshall. *Understanding Media: The Extensions of Man.* New York: McGraw Hill, 1964.

McLuhan, Marshall, and Quentin Fiore. *The Medium is the Message: An Inventory of Effects.* New York: Bantam, 1967.

Midgley, Mary. *Science as Salvation:A Modern Myth and Its Meaning (.* New York: Routledge, 1992.

Mumford, Lewis. *The Myth of the Machine: The Pentagon of Power.* New York: Harvest, 1970.

—. *The Myth of the Machine; Technics and Human Development.* New York: Harcourt Brace Jovanovich, 1966.

—. *The Transformations of Man .* New York: Collier, 1956.

Nisbet, Robert. *History of the Idea of Progress.* New York: Basic Books, 1980.

Noble, David F. *The Religion of Technology.* New York: Knopf, 1997.

—. *The Religion of Technology: The Divinity of Man and the Spirit of Invention.* New York: Knopf, 1997.

Orwell, George. "HBJ, Inc." *New York*, 1984: 17.

Pink. *"Perfect" in Greatest Hits...So Far!!!* . La Face Records, 2010.

Randall, Jr., John Herman. *The Making of the Modern Mind: A Survey of the Intellectual Background of the Present Age.* New York: Columbia University Press, 1976.

Smith, Huston (Eliot quoted in). *The World's Religions: Our Great Wisdom Traditions.* San Francisco: Harper, 1991.

Stock, Gregory. *Metaman: The Merging of Humans and Machines into a Global Superorganism.* New York: Simon and Schuster, 1993.

—. *Metaman: The Merging of Humans and Machines into a Global Superorganism.* New York: Simon and Schuster, 1993.

Terlizzese, Lawrence J. "Hope in the Thought of Jacques Ellul." *Cascade*, Eugene, OR: 104-105.

Tichi, Cecelia. *Shifting Gears: Technology, Literature, Culture in Modernist America.* Chapel Hill, NC: The University of North Carolina Press, 1987.

Tillich, Paul. *Systematic Theology: Reason and Revelation Being and God, Vol. 1.* Chicago: University of Chicago Press, 1951.

Volti, Rudi. *Society and Technological Change, 4th ed.* New York: Worth Publishers, 2001.

Wells, H.G. *The Time Machine.* New York: Bantam, 1895; 1982.

www.ingramcontent.com/pod-product-compliance
Lightning Source LLC
Chambersburg PA
CBHW031458040426
42444CB00007B/1140